ANGRY WHITE WOMAN

By Kramer Kelly

CLICHES & PHRASES

ELITE

Is there any film or TV hero who is not part of an 'elite' force? No. Because if you are not 'elite' you are not important enough. You are normal, you are average. You have nothing to live for or aspire to, unless you are about to accomplish something momentous and therefore now qualify for that 'elite' addendum to your name. Ho hum.

If the character is not a member of an 'elite' class to begin with, by the end of the piece he/she will be. You can take that for granted. 'Elite' is shorthand for VIP of skill or class distinction.

In any description in media, expect the word 'elite' to be applied. You should cringe. I know I do.

PERFECT STORM

Recently was added "it's a perfect storm" to the parlance of the day. But this is strictly a media shorthand, a given when at least two variables brought into play produce an outcome that may or may not have been pre-determined.

The news media love shorthand descriptive phrases that make them sound flip, as if they just learned it as the new IN word of the day and they have to issue it immediately, to be thought in the know, as if its usage denotes a gold star.

It's all wildly annoying and predictable and part of the reason people are bored with media talking heads.

BRUTALLY ALSO **SHOCKING**

You may have noticed that just about the only time you ever hear the word 'brutally' is when it's spoken by a news person and it will be followed by the word "murdered."

The other word used in the same context is 'shocking'.

The reason 'brutal' is so in use is because it is jarring and gets the audiences' attention. We have expectations based upon the callousness that word signifies to us. As a listener you immediately want to know how brutally the victim was murdered.

Mostly you are disappointed as it turns out to be an (unfortunately) routine slaying, such as a single gunshot wound or a knifing, with someone dying instantly or at least without grave suffering beforehand. Sometimes the murder seems even softly done, without any suffering to the victim. So this is 'brutal'? It is only in the context that any violent interference with another person can be considered 'brutal'.

With ho hum murder you wonder if there is something wrong with you for being disappointed.

But it's not YOU who raised your expectations. It's the media who did that. You expect 'brutal' to indicate something unexpected or truly shocking, a messy prolonged death or a torture victim or mass slaughter. It's that simple. Then you're supposed to feel ashamed because you didn't get that? But the news media hooked you with 'brutally' or 'shocking' and then didn't deliver. They didn't fulfil your expectations, based upon an ingrained notion of what is brutal and shocking and what is not.

What happens when 'shocking' and 'brutal' become so mundane that as an audience we no longer react to them? Is there a word to elevate to? Is 'heinous' next? And where do we go when that is no longer enough?

EMERGENCY NEWS BREAKING or BREAKING NEWS BULLETIN

Very often breaking news is nothing more than a repetition of what someone already said on-air or it is something excruciatingly mundane, like a perp walk into a courthouse, as if that was making the Earth standstill, or at least your own country. Instead of what it used to be: something equivalent to the death of a president, a landing on the moon, or a terrorist attack.

Nowadays the whole nation has to pay attention when another middle-class blonde girl goes missing. "We have breaking news, there is no news."

How many other women are missing and no one pays attention at all?

TSUNAMI

Tsunami is an interesting word because so many people use it only because it is so fun to say.

A tsunami sometimes goes hand-in-hand with a perfect storm for obvious reasons and can be used to describe the same combination of factors, the tsunami being the end result of the activity that comprised the perfect storm.

But how many people talk that way in real life? How often in business or in personal life does anyone say we have this and that and therefore we have this perfect storm and so this is a tsunami about to hit.

If you live in a tsunami zone you probably don't like the term being utilized so casually – even if it is fun to say.

SCHIZOPHRENIA

This is a condition that involves a true disengagement with reality. It is NOT Multiple Personality Disorder, though that's the common misconception. The terms schizoid and schizophrenic have been used so often to erroneously describe behavior in which two opposing attitudes are being exhibited, they have become misleading clichés when it is not.

Schizophrenia is about experiencing symptoms such as paranoia and hallucinations. That is NOT multiple personality disorder, except maybe if one of the other personalities inhabiting the psyche also happens to be schizophrenic. Now that would be fun: weird, but fun.

A newer term is Dissociative Identity Disorder. Which is not as much fun to say as Schizophrenia, I admit.

ANCHOR BABY

What is an anchor baby?

Is it for the immigrant who is here either illegally or legally and gives birth in a country where birthright citizenship is in place? Though this does not, by extension, give the parent citizenship.

Or is it a woman who gets pregnant by a man she is in a relationship with, tying him to her forever, no matter how their relationship rolls? What if this same woman keeps repeating that pattern with different men? Is she establishing anchor babies, not for citizenship but for access and maybe even for support and a sense of identity thru the father(s) of her kids?

Keep in mind the so-called anchor baby of an immigrant may have citizenship but the parents do not gain citizenship thru the status of their child.

THROWN UNDER THE BUS

How many people have you seen thrown under a bus? Evidently when someone blames someone else for a group failure, that person is thrown under the bus. That's rather drastlc, don't you think?

THROW THE BABY OUT WITH THE BATH WATER

This is a variation on 'throw the good out with the bad' and 'slicing off your nose to spite your face'. I mean, the baby reference is a little cruel, like a lot of those nursery rhymes so it's maybe not the best image.

SMOKING GUN

Looking into a scandal, this is what everyone is looking for. Not literally any smoking gun, of course.

THE JUDGES ARE GOING TO KILL ME

In certain competitions the contestants really exaggerate. I mean, really kill you? Whatever. You'll live through it.

I'M GUTTED

Do you ever use this one? It is a British way of describing a personal disappointment. I'm certain any being literally gutted would be insulted by this description. Go get yourself a cup of tea and get over it.

A GRAND JURY WILL INDICT A HAM SANDWICH

Wow. Can you be any more insulting to a jury? However it is true the prosecution steers the jury to whatever outcome the prosecutor wants. Which means when a jury doesn't indict, the prosecutor probably never wanted it.

DREAM TEAM

Any group of two or more people who comprise a select group of talent. Just remember your dream could be someone else's nightmare.

HOLY GRAIL

Someone is always looking for this, I mean the real one. But the phrase has been adapted to describe any item of perceived value that is difficult to get one's hands on. So it doesn't matter if you are looking for a piece of art or any type of historical artifact. In fact you can have a multitude of holy grail items being sought at any given time on any given list. The overuse of the term has become inane.

ANGRY BLACK WOMAN

All black women are perceived as having an attitude, I guess. Like they used to be perceived as expert in arousing a man's sexual passion - at least if you asked their white masters. So from a one-time sexual threat, a black woman has now evolved into being an angry threat?

OUR THOUGHTS AND PRAYERS ARE WITH YOU

Is this a shorthand phrase? It seems totally acceptable as a blithe official response to a tragedy but totally meaningless as well.

SHORT COMMENTARIES ON THINGS THAT DRIVE ME CRAZY

SKEPTICS

THERE IS A DIFFERENCE BETWEEN OPEN-MINDED AND CLOSE-MINDED SKEPTICS. A CLOSE-MINDED SKEPTIC IS UNABLE TO LEARN ANYTHING NEW. SO TO THOSE WHO SCOFF AT THE INTELLECTUAL CURIOSITY OF OTHERS, REMEMBER YOU ARE THE ONE EXHIBITING STUNTED GROWTH. IN FACT, IF YOU DON'T WANT TO SEE ANYTHING PARANORMAL, YOU WON'T. BUT IF YOU DON'T EXPECT TO SEE ANYTHING PARANORMAL, YOU WILL.

VIOLENT VIDEO GAMES

BREEDING SOCIOPATHS. THE PARENTS OF THESE KIDS DON'T HAVE A PROBLEM WITH THAT. THEY THINK IT'S A NEW FORM OF TELEVISION, HENCE A NEW BABYSITTER. SINCE KILLING PEOPLE AND ANIMALS IS THE PRIMARY GOAL OF THESE VIDEO GAMES — USUALLY ARMED CONFLICT — YOU'D

THINK SOMETHING WOULD CONNECT IN THE MINDS OF THE PARENTS, AND IT'S BOTHERSOME IT DOESN'T.

OPEN CARRY & GUN NUTS

THERE IS A JOKE THAT ONLY GUYS WITH SMALL PENISES NEED CARRY BIG GUNS OR ANY GUNS FOR THAT MATTER. BUT THESE ARE FREEDOM-LOVING TERRORISTS, TERRORIZING THEIR FELLOW CITIZENS. THEY SEEK TO INTIMIDATE PEOPLE WHO DON'T SHARE THEIR PHILOSOPHY, LIVING OUT SOME FANTASY OF BEING IN THE WILD WEST, WHICH WAS NOT A ROMANTIC – OR EVEN VERY HYGIENIC – PLACE TO BE, THOUGH THAT'S A STORY ALL ITS OWN.

IN THEIR MINDS THESE BULLIES PROJECT AN IMAGE OF SUPERHERO STATUS.

BUT WOULD A GROUP OF GUN NUTS WELCOME A MAN OR WOMAN OF COLOR TO WALK THE

STREETS OR PATRONIZE STORES OR OCCUPY GOVERNMENT BUILDINGS WITH THEM? OF COURSE NOT, SINCE THE MAIN REASON FOR THE EXHIBITION OF WHITE SUPER-POWER IS TO INTIMIDATE THE GOVERNMENT (A FORM OF TREASON, IF YOU WILL) AND ESPECIALLY PEOPLE OF COLOR WHO DEMAND EQUAL RIGHTS. YOU MIGHT CONSIDER THE DIRECT LINE OF LINEAGE TO BE KKK TO PRESENT-DAY GUN NUTS.

REFLECT ON HOW TREASONOUS ANTI-FEDERAL GOVERNMENT ADVOCATES TOOK OVER TERRITORY IN NEVADA AND OREGON, WITH LAW ENFORCEMENT BACKING DOWN RATHER THAN RISKING BLOODSHED. COMPARE THAT TO PEACEFUL PROTESTS IN CITIES WHERE PEOPLE OF COLOR ARE DEMANDING RESPECT AND EQUAL TREATMENT UNDER THE LAW ONLY TO BE MET WITH TANKS AND PEPPER SPRAY AND CURFEWS.

IS AN OPEN CARRY CRUSADER OR LAW ENFORCEMENT OFFICIAL ALL THAT HAPPY IF THE PERSON OPENLY CARRYING A GUN IS A MAN OF COLOR?

MISTRESSES

ISN'T A MISTRESS OF A MAN A WOMAN WHO IS BEING FINANCIALLY SUPPORTED BY HIM? SHOULDN'T A WOMAN HAVING A PHYSICAL RELATIONSHIP WITH A MARRIED MAN BE KNOWN AS A GIRLFRIEND OR AN ASSOCIATE WHEN HE IS NOT PAYING HER BILLS? YET THE WOMAN WHO IS HAVING AN AFFAIR WITH A MARRIED MAN IS ALWAYS TERMED HIS MISTRESS, NO MATTER HER PERSONAL INDEPENDENCE.

IT BUGS ME WHEN A WOMAN WITH WHOM A MAN IS HAVING AN AFFAIR IS IDENTIFIED AS HIS

MISTRESS, AS IF HE OWNS HER. SHE IS NOT HIS POSSESSION.

COMPARE THIS TO A MAN WHO IS HAVING AN AFFAIR WITH A MARRIED WOMAN. WHAT DO YOU CALL HIM — A MASTER? OF COURSE NOT. IF HE IS BEING SUPPORTED BY HER, HE IS A GIGOLO, BUT IF NOT BEING SUPPORTED BY HER HE IS SIMPLY THE MAN SHE IS HAVING AN AFFAIR WITH, A LOVER.

TASTE OVER FLAVOR

TASTING IS A FUNCTION, WHILE FLAVOR IS WHAT SOMETHING TASTES LIKE. NOWADAYS NO ONE USES THE WORD FLAVOR, THEY SUBSTITUTE TASTE FOR EVERYTHING, IN ALL THE TV ADS IT IS ABOUT THIS FOOD ITEM HAVING "GREAT TASTE."

SO NOW YOU NOT ONLY TASTE A PRODUCT, YOU HAVE TO LIKE THE TASTE OF IT, INSTEAD OF

TASTING SOMETHING AND THEN APPRECIATING THE FLAVOR OF IT. WHY AND HOW DID THE WORD TASTE REPLACE THE WORD FLAVOR?

RELIGIOUS FUNDAMENTALISTS

RELIGIOUS CONSERVATIVES OF ANY KIND ARE BAD NEWS TO THE REST OF US. NOT ONLY ARE THEY RESTRICTIVE AND JUDGMENTAL TYPES, BUT THEY ROUTINELY SEEK TO BRAINWASH THE YOUNG INTO HAVING EXACTLY THE SAME ATTITUDES. AND ALL FUNDAMENTALISTS ARE THE SAME, WHICH MEANS THEY DO NOT TOLERATE OTHER FUNDAMENTALISTS. IT IS VERY DIFFICULT TO EVEN HOLD A CONVERSATION WITH ANY OF THEM UNLESS YOU ARE COMPLETELY OF LIKE MIND.

JEWS, CHRISTIANS AND MUSLIMS WORSHIP THE SAME GOD BUT YOU WOULD NOT KNOW THEY ARE SEPARATE BRANCHES FROM THE SAME TREE

BY THE WAY THEY TREAT EACH OTHER. YES, EACH BRANCH HAS THEIR OWN PROPHETS (CHRISTIANS TAKE IT ONE STEP FURTHER, CLAIMING THEIR PROPHET TO BE THE SON OF GOD) BUT MUST THEY CONSTANTLY FIND THEMSELVES IN CONFLICT WITH EACH OTHER? IT SEEMS THEY JUST CAN'T GET ALONG, AND UNFORTUNATELY THEIR HATRED CONSUMES THE ENTIRE WORLD.

IN THE U.S. THE EVANGELICAL CONTINGENT IS ALSO RABIDLY DEVOTED TO ISRAEL. FOR THE SAKE OF THE SECOND COMING, ISRAEL MUST BE STANDING. THEY PROFESS A DEVOTION TO ISRAEL SO DEVOUT IT IS ALARMING THEY MAY FLY THE STARS AND STRIPES WHEN IT'S REALLY THE ISRAEL FLAG THEY SHOULD BE SALUTING.

FINALLY, ANY DENOMINATION OF FUNDAMENTALISM IN THE CHRISTIAN, JEWISH

OR MUSLIM COMMUNITIES IS AS BAD AS THE OTHER.

OLD WHITE MEN

THE SUPREME COURT OF THE UNITED STATES IS MAINLY OCCUPIED BY CONSERVATIVE WHITE MEN COMPLETELY OUT OF TOUCH WITH THE REAL WORLD AS THEY LIVE IN SUCH A PROTECTED ENVIRONMENT.

DID YOU KNOW PROTESTERS ARE LEGALLY BARRED FROM THE STEPS OF THE COURT BUILDING, PREVENTING THEM FROM EVEN GETTING CLOSE TO ONE OF THESE PRIVILEGED GUYS? (YET ANTI-ABORTIONISTS ARE ALLOWED TO GET RIGHT INTO THE FACE OF ANY WOMAN WALKING INTO A CLINIC THAT OFFERS ABORTION SERVICES, AND THE REASON FOR THIS? ACCORDING TO THE SUPREME COURT IT IS A MATTER OF FREE SPEECH.)

THESE PIPSQUEAK LITTLE MEN MAKE PRONOUNCEMENTS THAT LARGELY WILL PROVE EMBARRASSING TO THEM, AND IF YOU DON'T BELIEVE THAT, JUST TRY READING SOME OF THEIR OPINIONS.

PATRIARCHAL SOCIETY

THE LONG STANDING PATRIARCHAL SOCIETY OF THE UNITED STATES IS FIGHTING DESPERATELY TO WITHSTAND THE ONSLAUGHT OF FEMALE AUTONOMY.

IF YOU DON'T BELIEVE ME, THINK ABOUT THE RESTRICTIONS ON ABORTION AND EVEN FEMALE-SPECIFIC MEDICAL CARE THAT HAS BEEN MAKING ITS WAY THROUGH THE MAJORITY OF THE STATES. (THOSE STATES ARE GENERALLY IN REPUBLICAN PARTY CONTROL.)

REMEMBER THE RIGHT FOR A WOMAN TO SEEK LEGAL ABORTION WAS DECIDED BY THE

SUPREME COURT (A CONSERVATIVE COURT) MANY DECADES AGO.

WHAT IS ALL THIS CONSERVATIVE MALE ACTION ABOUT? IS IT BECAUSE MEN WANT TO RULE ON EVERYTHING, EVEN WHETHER A WOMAN HAS SEX? THIS IS MALE PATRIARCHY VERSUS ANY ATTEMPT AT FEMALE AUTONOMY, WHETHER ON THE WORK FRONT OR IN THE BEDROOM.

CHINESE RESTAURANTS

I LOVE CHINESE FOOD. BUT BE CAREFUL. KEEP TO VEGETARIAN CUISINE. HARD TO DO WHEN YOU'RE IN CHINA, I KNOW.

RECYCLING

TRASHY PEOPLE TRASH AND THAT INCLUDES THOSE WHO LITTER. PEOPLE WHO LITTER OR DON'T RECYCLE HAVE A FUNDAMENTAL LACK OF

RESPECT FOR THE ENVIRONMENT AND FELLOW HUMANS.

AND WHY IS IT MAINLY WHITE PEOPLE IN URBAN AREAS WHO RECYCLE? WHY IS IT EVERYONE ELSE SEEMS TO THINK THE LAND THEY STAND UPON IS A DUMPING SITE?

LIBERTARIANS

LIBERTARIANS ARE ALL OVER THE PLACE. THEY ABHOR ANY INFRINGEMENT UPON PERSONAL FREEDOM. BUT THEY LARGELY SUPPORT SEATBELTS. WHY? WHY ISN'T IT AN INDIVIDUAL OPTION WHETHER A DRIVER OR PASSENGER WEARS SEATBELTS OR NOT? ISN'T IT A HUMAN RIGHT TO DECIDE ON WHETHER TO TAKE SUPPLEMENTS, EXERCISE OR ANYTHING ELSE PRESUMABLY HEALTHY FOR YOUR BODY? WHY SHOULD SEATBELTS BE DIFFERENT? MY WEARING A SEATBELT DOES NOT IMPACT ANY

OTHER DRIVER ON THE ROAD, WHETHER OR NOT WE ARE IN AN ACCIDENT.

IF YOU CLAIM THIS REDUCES INSURANCE COSTS OVERALL, CAN YOU PROVE THAT SAVINGS TO THE CUSTOMER?

POLLUTION

POLLUTION MAKES YOU DIRTY, BOTH IN YOUR BODY AND OUTSIDE YOUR BODY. WE SHOULD DO ALL WE CAN TO ELIMINATE POLLUTION AND THAT MEANS CLEAN AIR AND CLEAN WATER AND CLEAN FOOD. THAT MEANS ANTI-POLLUTION ENERGY SUCH AS WIND FARMS AND SOLAR. THAT ALSO MEANS ELIMINATING THE USE OF OIL AND COAL (WHICH IN NO WAY WAS EVER 'CLEAN COAL' AS FIRST ADVERTISED BACK IN THE LATE 1800s). IN THE PROCESS OF GETTING RID OF THE DIRT THAT MAKES US ALL FILTHY WE WILL BE

SAVING THE PLANET FOR OURSELVES AND OUR DESCENDANTS, AND THAT IS NOT A BAD THING.

ARE YOU HELPING OR ARE YOU PART OF THE PROBLEM?

PASSIVE PEOPLE ARE THE WORST. THEY ARE OF NO USE TO ANYONE AT ANY TIME. THEY WAIT FOR OTHER PEOPLE TO DO THEIR THINKING FOR THEM.

PASSIVE PEOPLE ARE LAZY.

AND IF YOU DON'T VOTE, YOU HAVE NO RIGHT TO COMPLAIN AT ALL. BUT DON'T VOTE IF YOU HAVE NO IDEA WHAT'S REALLY GOING ON. BUT WHY WOULD YOU BE PROUD OF THAT?

THE AMERICAN PEOPLE HAVE SPOKEN

WHO CARES? MOST OF THEM ARE STUPID. THEY CAN'T EVEN NAME THE BRANCHES OF GOVERNMENT. THEY HAVE TROUBLE NAMING

THE PRESIDENT OF THE UNITED STATES DURING WORLD WAR II AND THERE WERE TWO OF THEM!

THE DEATH PENALTY

IF NOT IN PLAY FOR UNDER EXCEPTIONAL CIRCUMSTANCE, IT IS MERELY AN EXHIBITION FOR A RAVENING HERD OF SADISTIC BEASTS, GETTING THEIR OWN REVENGE UPON THE WORLD IN THE APPLICATION OF THIS ROMAN CIRCUS. SEND THE CULPRIT TO THE GUILLOTINE! THE GAS CHAMBER! THE FIRING SQUAD!

GREED

ESPECIALLY WHEN IT EXHIBITS ANTI-SOCIETAL TENDENCIES, GREED EQUATES TO THE MOST ANTI-SOCIAL BEHAVIOR, AS IN "I'VE GOT MINE, SO FUCK YOU!"

GREEDY PEOPLE ARE OFTEN AYN RAND FANATICS, AND THE PHILOSOPHY OF AYN RAND IS ADOPTED BY SELFISH PEOPLE LOOKING FOR JUSTIFICATION FOR THEIR SELFISHNESS. IT'S NOT A SURPRISE MOST PEOPLE GET INTO THIS PHILOSOPHY WHEN THEY ARE TEENAGERS. WHO IS MORE SELF-INVOLVED THAN A TEENAGER? AYN RAND GIVES YOU AN EXCUSE TO REMAIN A TEENAGER FOR THE REST OF YOUR LIFE.

TEXAS

ONE STAR IS ALL IT'S WORTH.

RESEARCH SCIENTISTS

SADISTS BECOME RESEARCH SCIENTISTS SO THEY CAN LEGALLY INFLICT TORTURE UPON LIVE SUBJECTS.

SPORTS FANS

SEE DEATH PENALTY, RESEARCH SCIENTISTS AND GREED.

GEORGE W BUSH, #43

THE WORST PRESIDENT OF THE UNITED STATES, EVER. THAT TAKES SOME DOING. IF YOU DON'T AGREE, TRY TUNING INTO REALITY FOR A CHANGE.

HE STARTED TWO WARS, AND WAS WRONG ABOUT BOTH OF THEM. HE WANTED CONTROL OF A LOT OF OIL AND DIDN'T GET IT. A LOT OF PEOPLE DIED. HE EVEN SPOKE AT AN EVENT FOR VETERANS OF THOSE WARS AND POCKETED THE CASH INSTEAD OF DONATING IT. HE PAINTS PICTURES OF HIMSELF OR LEADERS HE USED TO KNOW, TO REMIND US OF HIS FORMER GLORY.

HE WAS MOM'S FAVORITE BOY, BECAUSE MOMS ALWAYS LOVE THE BAD BOY BEST. SHE SHOULD HAVE NOTICED HE HAD BEADY EYES.

NEVER TRULY ELECTED (FLORIDA 2000 & OHIO 2004) HE MANAGED TO FINAGLE THE PRESIDENCY FOR TWO EXCRUCIATING TERMS.

HE MAINTAINS POPULARITY WITH THE DEAF, DUMB AND BLIND AND THE EVANGELICAL FOLKS, WHO FUNCTION THE SAME. GOD SPARE US FROM THE EVANGELICAL VOTER.

EVANGELICALS

GOD SPARE US FROM THEM. THEY INSIST ON TAKING THE OLD TESTAMENT LITERALLY EVEN THOUGH THE JEWS DO NOT, WHICH IS WHY IT IS CONSTANTLY BEING REINTERPRETED.

THEY BELIEVE JESUS RODE ON A DINOSAUR AND THE EXODUS FROM EGYPT OCCURRED EXACTLY AS THEY HAVE SEEN IT IN A MOVIE.

DO THEY EVEN KNOW THE TRUE CROSS WAS LIKELY AN X SHAPE RATHER THAN A T? OF COURSE NOT, AS TRUE HISTORY HAS NO PLACE IN THEIR MINDS OR HEARTS.

A TRUE BELIEVER IN CHRIST WOULD DOUBT AND QUESTION AND FIND ANSWERS AND BE SATISFIED, BELIEVING DESPITE THE LACK OF TRUE EVIDENCE. BUT EVANGELICALS DO NOT BELIEVE IN QUESTIONING, MAKING THEIR SO-CALLED TRUE BELIEF A WEAKNESS RATHER THAN A STRENGTH. THEY DARE NOT BE TESTED, YOU SEE.

THEY MIGHT WANT TO READ UP ON BISHOP SPONG'S WORKS AS WELL. ESPECIALLY USEFUL ARE HIS EXPLANATIONS ON HOW THE BIBLE'S

QUOTATIONS HAVE BEEN MISINTERPRETED. THE RED SEA IS REALLY THE REED SEA, FOR INSTANCE, LIKELY A MARSHLAND. AND IT WASN'T REALLY 'A CAMEL THROUGH THE HEAD OF A NEEDLE' EITHER.

ABORTION

ABORTION IS THE MOST CONTROVERSIAL DEFINING ISSUE OF THE CENTURY - THIS ONE OR THE LAST. YOU WOULD THINK ROWE VS WADE SETTLED THE ISSUE DECADES AGO. (ABORTION IS NOT EVEN A POLITICAL POINT OF DEBATE IN OTHER WESTERN CULTURES.) YET THE ANTI-ABORTION CONTINGENT MOUNTS SMEAR CAMPAIGNS OF FALSE DATA, EMPLOYS INTIMIDATION TACTICS AND EVEN CONDONES THE MURDERING OF PHYSICIANS WHO ENABLE THIS LEGAL AND SAFE MEDICAL PROCEDURE.

YET THE CORE ISSUE IS WOMEN HAVE THE RIGHT TO DICTATE WHAT HAPPENS WITHIN THEIR BODIES.

NO OTHER PERSON SHOULD INFLICT THEIR WILL OVER ANOTHER, ESPECIALLY WHEN THEY HAVE NO PERSONAL OR FINANCIAL STAKE IN THE CONSEQUENCES. YET THESE PEOPLE WOULD MAKE A GIRL OR WOMAN CARRY A BABY TO FULL TERM, YET ARE REMOVED FROM THE CONSEQUENCES TO BOTH MOTHER AND CHILD. HOW FAIR IS THAT?

AND THESE SAME PEOPLE OFTEN WANT TO DENY WOMEN CONTRACEPTIVES. THIS PROVES THEIR REAL MOTIVATION IS TO MAKE WOMEN ASHAMED THEY HAVE SEX, LET ALONE HAVING IT ON THEIR OWN TERMS.

SOME PEOPLE EVEN WANT TO RE-INSTITUTE SHAMING TACTICS, MEANING A WOMAN

SEEKING AN ABORTION MUST PUBLICIZE THE NAME OF EVERY LOVER SHE HAS HAD EVEN WHEN IT HAS NO RELEVANCE. IF THIS SOUNDS RIDICULOUS, KEEP IN MIND IT IS AN EXAMPLE OF THE PATRIARCHAL SYSTEM.

ADD A WOMAN'S STONING INTO THE MIX, AND YOU HAVE A GOOD EXAMPLE OF ISLAMIC FUNDAMENTALISM.

A PRO-CHOICE PERSON IS SAYING IT IS AN INDIVIDUAL'S CHOICE WHETHER TO CONTINUE OR TERMINATE A PREGNANCY, NO MATTER HOW THAT PREGNANCY CAME ABOUT. TO THINK OTHERWISE IS THE ULTIMATE DISRESPECT.

WHAT'S NORMAL?

IS THERE SUCH A THING AS NORMAL ANYMORE? IS BEING NORMAL SO UNFASHIONABLE, THAT WE HAVE TO COME UP WITH NEW TERMS AND CREATE PSYCHOSIS? ARE WE SUPPOSED TO BE

ASHAMED IF WE ARE NOT BEING TREATED FOR SOME MENTAL OR EMOTIONAL ABERRATION, FOR EVERY PERCEIVED EMOTIONAL INSTABILITY?

BI-POLAR ANYTHING SEEMS TO BE ALL THE RAGE. THAT AND AUTISM. FUN WORDS TO SAY, REALLY, MAKES YOU SOUND SMART JUST SAYING THOSE WORDS. JUST ABOUT ANYTHING COMES UNDER THIS BANNER, TOO.

SHYNESS IS NOW ASPERGER'S INSTEAD OF THE SOCIAL AWKWARDNESS THAT USED TO BE THOUGHT ENDEARING, ESPECIALLY IN GOOD-LOOKING MEN OR WOMEN. NOW IT'S A FORM OF AUTISM. IT SEEMS WE'VE GONE BACKWARDS IN FINDING SOCIAL ACCEPTABILITY. WHY CAN'T SOMEONE JUST BE SHY?

BASIC BI-POLAR IS A LACK OF SELF-CONTROL, EITHER IN TEMPERAMENT OR EXHIBITING MANIC-DEPRESSIVE BEHAVIOR.

WHAT THIS ALL COMES DOWN TO IS EXCUSES, AND A MEDICAL DIAGNOSIS TO ALLOW FOR MEDICATION.

THIS EQUATES TO SELF-INDULGENT CAPITALIST TREATS TO THE PHARMACEUTICAL INDUSTRY, WHO CLEANS UP WITH ALL THE PRESCRIPTIONS.

THIS IS A DEPENDENCY COP-OUT, A SELF-INDULGENT WAY OF EXCUSING OUR OWN LAZINESS OR LACK OF WILL OR EVEN LACK OF CHARACTER.

THIS ALSO CONFUSES THE ISSUE FOR PEOPLE WHO HAVE GENUINE ILLNESSES WHO REQUIRE MEDICATION TO REMAIN VITAL. HOW MANY PEOPLE SUSPECT THESE VICTIMS ARE FAKING IT BECAUSE SO MANY PEOPLE HAVE THE DISEASE-OF-THE-DAY?

WHEN ILLNESS BECOMES COMMONPLACE, FASHIONABLE, OR TAKEN FOR GRANTED – AN

OFF-HAND, CASUAL DIAGNOSIS — WE ARE ALL IN DANGER OF BEING TAKEN FOR GRANTED, MISUNDERSTOOD OR OVER-MEDICATED.

MODERN PARENTING

THE WAY CHILDREN USED TO BE RAISED, OUT OF SIGHT OF THEIR PARENTS AS THEY PLAYED IN THE STREET OR PARK OR SCHOOL YARD OR AT THEIR FRIENDS' HOUSES, IS NOW CONSIDERED NEGLECT.

TOYS THAT USED TO BE TAKEN FOR GRANTED, LIKE JACKS OR PICK-UP-STICKS, ARE NOW CONSIDERED SO DANGEROUS (THOUGH I NEVER HEARD OF ONE KID WHO EVER GOT HURT) SOME STORES REFUSE TO SELL THEM.

DID YOU KNOW THERE WAS SUCH A THING AS A LATCH-KEY KID AND NO ONE THOUGHT ANYTHING ABOUT IT? MANY KIDS GOT THEMSELVES TO SCHOOL AND HOME AGAIN

WITHOUT ANY UNDUE DRAMA (OR TRAUMA), JUST LIFE AS USUAL. NOWADAYS IF A KID IS WALKING HALF A BLOCK HOME FROM THE PARK GUESS WHAT? A NEIGHBOR CALLS THE COPS AND SOCIAL SERVICES IS BROUGHT IN. IT'S A SHAME.

BUT NOWADAYS PARENTS ARE A BIG PART OF THE PROBLEM. THEY ARE MAKING THEIR KIDS TOO DEPENDENT ON THEM. THE CHILD HAS NO SENSE OF INDEPENDENCE AT ANY POINT IN HIS LIFE. WHY SHOULD HE/SHE?

THE FACT IS THE CHILD IS NEVER FAR FROM THE PARENTAL EYE, ESPECIALLY WITH OLD HOUSES' INTERIOR WALLS COMING DOWN TO PROMOTE THE 'OPEN CONCEPT' THAT EVEN CLASSIC VICTORIANS MUST CEDE TO. WHEN I CATCH A RENOVATION SHOW, THAT IS THE NUMBER ONE REQUEST, SOME OPEN CONCEPT SO THE PARENT CAN KEEP A CONSTANT EYE UPON THE CHILD.

WHY? WHAT DO THESE PARENTS FEAR WILL HAPPEN TO THEIR CHILD IF IT'S PLAYING IN THAT OTHER ROOM IN THE HOUSE?

THIS OVER-PROTECTIVENESS IS NOT RATIONAL, UNLESS IT IS A WAY FOR THE PARENT TO OVER-COMPENSATE FOR THE TRUE LACK OF QUALITY TIME SPENT WITH THE CHILD IN THE FIRST PLACE.

SPYING ON THE CHILD AND SPENDING BIG MONEY ON GIFTS WILL NOT COMPENSATE FOR TRULY GREAT PARENTING AND TRULY GREAT PARENTING DOES NOT EQUATE TO THE OTHER TWO.

ON THE OTHER HAND, AT LEAST THE PARENTS ARE DOING SOMETHING FOR THEIR CHILD, AND THAT IS ENCOURAGING JUNIOR PRINCE OR PRINCESS TO THINK THE ENTIRE WORLD REVOLVES AROUND THEM.

GOOD WORK, PARENTS!

WEALTH MANAGEMENT ADS

ALWAYS SHOWCASE WHITE MIDDLE-CLASS LOOKING COUPLES. HAVE YOU NOTICED THAT? AND THE USE OF THE WORD WEALTH IS ALSO TELLING. IT'S SAYING WHITE PEOPLE SHOULD BE WEALTHY, EVERYONE IS OR SHOULD BE WEALTHY, WHICH MAKES YOU FEEL BAD IF YOU ARE NOT, LIKE YOU MISSED OUT ON SOMETHING.

PARLIAMENTARY SYSTEM

I'M NOT TALKING ABOUT A MONARCHY OR PEOPLE YELLING AT SOMEONE IN A PIT — THE BRITISH EXAMPLE.

BUT THE FAILURE OF THE TWO-PARTY SYSTEM IN THE U.S. (THE FOUNDERS NEVER WANTED A TWO-PARTY SYSTEM ANYWAY) AND WHAT THE SITUATION HAS DEGRADED TO MEANS WE SHOULD CONSIDER OTHER OPTIONS.

A PARLIAMENTARY SYSTEM FOR THE U.S. COULD ADAPT THE TWO-PARTY SYSTEM AND BRING IT UP TO DATE, MINUS A MONARCHY, BUT WITH THE PLUSES INTACT.

EACH PARTY RUNS TO HEAD THE GOVERNMENT AND IT'S A WINNER TAKES ALL APPROACH. THE LOSER HAS NO SAY WHATSOEVER IN WHAT HAPPENS IN GOVERNMENT, THEY CAN ONLY TAKE TO COMPLAINING A LOT AND MAYBE THROWING TANTRUMS, BUT CHILDISH OBSTRUCTIONISM DOESN'T MAKE ANY DIFFERENCE.

THE HEAD OF THE PARTY BECOMES THE PRESIDENT. IF SOMETHING BAD HAPPENS AND THAT PERSON HAS TO STEP DOWN, THE NEXT IN LINE BECOMES THE PRESIDENT.

IF THE PARTY ITSELF HAS REALLY SCREWED UP THEN A SPECIAL ELECTION IS CALLED AND THE PEOPLE VOTE YET AGAIN!

AND THE EVEN GREATER NEWS IS THE VOTING CYCLE IS APPROXIMATELY FIVE WEEKS, MINUS BIG MONEY TV ADS AND ONLY ONE PRIMARY. SHORT ATTENTION-SPAN SWEET, JUST AS AMERICANS LIKE IT!

PEOPLE WHO HATE ANIMALS

USUALLY FINDING DEER A NUISANCE AND DOGS TOO NOISY AND CATS TOO INDEPENDENT AND BIRDS TOO... WHATEVER. RABBITS, RACCOONS, THESE PEOPLE HATE THEM ALL. WHY? THAT'S EASY. THEY LOATHE ANYTHING OUTSIDE OF THEIR CONTROL. IT IS THE ULTIMATE DISPLAY OF EGOMANIA.

JUST BECAUSE YOU CAN DOESN'T MEAN YOU SHOULD

THIS SHOULD BE SELF-EVIDENT. JUST BECAUSE YOU ARE CAPABLE OF SOMETHING DOESN'T MEAN THAT'S SOMETHING YOU SHOULD DO. TRY TO THINK ETHICALLY; TRY TO THINK OF WHAT IS THE BEST THING TO DO. TRY AND REMOVE YOUR EGO FROM THE EQUATION. AND TRY NOT TO MAKE LIFE TOO COMPLICATED. REMEMBER IF A CHEF HAS TO EXPLAIN A DISH TO A DINER IT'S NOT A GOOD DISH.

HOMESCHOOLING

IT'S HARD TO USE THE TERM HOMESCHOOLING WITHOUT ENCLOSING IT WITHIN QUOTATION MARKS. THAT'S HOW YOU THINK OF IT, RIGHT? "HOMESCHOOLING". SOMEONE IS BEING "HOMESCHOOLED". IN SHORT, PROBABLY A CHILD MEANT TO REMAIN AT HOME WITHIN AN

EXTREMELY SELECT SOCIETY TO PREVENT CONTAMINATION WITH VIEWPOINTS NOT APPROVED BY DISAPPROVING PARENTS. IN THE 21ST CENTURY, IS ANY EVOLVING INDUSTRY LIKELY TO EMPLOY SOMEONE WITH "HOMESCHOOLED" ON THEIR RESUME?

REPUBLICANS

REPUBLICANS USED TO BE FAIRLY REASONABLE. I MEAN, I'M SURE DEMOCRATS DIDN'T FEEL AT WAR WITH THEM. PROBABLY MEMBERS OF OPPOSING PARTIES WERE EVEN ALLOWED — IN THE MOST LIBERAL WINGS — TO CO-EXIST IN THE SAME FAMILY. BUT SINCE A CERTAIN BUSH VS GORE CALAMITY AND THEN A LATER BLACK MAN AS PRESIDENT AND ALL THE WHITE AGITATORS WHO RESENT A BLACK PRESIDENT OCCUPYING THIS MOST SACRED OFFICE, WELL, LET'S PUT IT THIS WAY. IF THE OBAMA ADMINISTRATION SOMEHOW FOUND A CURE FOR CANCER, THEY

WOULD ONLY RAIL AGAINST HIM FOR WASTING HIS EFFORTS ON CANCER INSTEAD OF HEART DISEASE. IT IS THAT SAD, AND REMARKABLY THAT TRAGIC. BUT THEN CANCER IS SUCH AN ELITIST THING, ISN'T IT? PROBABLY ONLY AFFLICTED BY THOSE LIBERAL DEMOCRATS.

THE NRA AKA NATIONAL RIFLE ASSOCIATION

THIS USED TO BE A RESPONSIBLE ORGANIZATION. BUT THAT WAS WHEN THE NRA WORKED FOR THE MEMBERSHIP AND NOT AS THE INTERMEDIARY FOR THE GUN MANUFACTURERS.

BACK WHEN HUNTING AS SPORT DECLINED, THE GUN SALES WERE GOING DOWN, SO THE MANUFACTURERS OF ARMS KNEW THEY HAD TO THRIVE BY STIMULATING SALES. STIMULATING SALES MEANT STIMULATING HEARTS — BY FEAR.

WITH YEARS SPENT BLOCKING SENSIBLE GUN CONTROL LEGISLATION AND WRITING NEW LEGISLATION PREVENTING RESTRICTIONS ON GUN OWNERSHIP, THE BEST THING THAT HAPPENED TO THE MANUFACTURERS AND THEREFORE THE NRA WAS THE ELECTION OF A BLACK PRESIDENT.

THE FEAR THE COUNTRY WAS BEING TAKEN AWAY FROM THEM MADE MANY WHITE PEOPLE GO GUN CRAZY, MEANING MORE CRAZY ABOUT GUNS, AND JUST PLAIN CRAZY.

DISTRUSTING THEIR GOVERNMENT IN THE HANDS OF A NON-WHITE (PERCEIVED) NON-CHRISTIAN, A CERTAIN MILITANT FACTION SOUGHT TO TAKE UP ARMS AGAINST THEIR GOVERNMENT, SWEARING ALLEGIANCE TO THE FLAG WHILE THEY SOUGHT TO OVERCOME IT.

HOW IS IT THEY DON'T REALIZE THEIR PATRIOTISM AMOUNTS TO TREASON AND THEIR ACTS AS TERRORISM?

WITH THE RUCKUS, GUN SALES HIT THE ROOF AND STAYED HIGH. THIS SMALLER NUMBER OF COMMITTED PEOPLE KEPT BUYING MORE AND MORE GUNS. IT'S LIKE A CHILD COLLECTING MORE TOYS.

THEY'RE FEELING SEXY ABOUT THE TOY, FEELING POWERFUL AND SEXY HOLDING A GUN, AS IF IT WEREN'T A WEAPON BUT AN APPENDAGE.

WHEN A MASS SHOOTING OCCURS THE NRA SAYS EVERYONE SHOULD HAVE A GUN, WHICH IS PLAIN LUNACY TO ANY SANE PERSON, AND YET A CERTAIN SEGMENT OF A SEGMENTED POPULATION BUYS INTO THAT, BUYS INTO BUYING MORE GUNS.

So with all the showmanship the manufacturers win as does the NRA, but do the people win? When you are just made more and more afraid in order to aid the single manufacturing unit (guns) that can't be sued — legally — are you really happy about this? Aren't you aware — you gun buyers, you — that you are being used and taken advantage of and being manipulated? Oh, maybe you are, but you just don't care.

WHY DO WE CALL IT ENTRÉE?

In Britain the three meal courses are STARTER, MAIN (COURSE) & DESSERT. In the U.S. there is appetizer, entrée & dessert. What's that about? It is a French word meaning 'entrance'. What does that have to do with the main course of a meal? Someone should write a book

ON THAT. THERE MIGHT BE SOME SUBVERSIVE ELEMENT TO IT. MAYBE WE DEVELOPED 'FRENCH FRIES' FOR FRIED POTATOES AS SOME TWISTED REVENGE.

INJUSTICE TO ANIMALS

O CANADA!

WHOA CANADA! THEY REALLY LIKE ANIMALS UP THERE, LIKE THEM DEAD THAT IS. FROM CLUBBING BABY SEALS TO DEATH OR IMPORTING DOG, CAT AND EVERY OTHER KIND OF FUR FROM CHINA, THERE'S A WICKED UNDERCURRENT TO ALL THE SMILES AND GOOD MANNERS.

DOWN PILLOWS & COMFORTERS

DID YOU KNOW THAT BIRDS ARE PLUCKED AND REPLUCKED UP TO SEVEN TIMES, THEIR SKIN NEVER HEALING, BARE-SKINNED TO THE ELEMENTS AND SCARRED, FINALLY DYING FROM THE TRAUMA? AND YOU REALLY NEED THIS PRODUCT TO FEEL WARM OR LUXURIOUS? THIS IS NOT A LUXURY; THIS IS AN EXAMPLE OF DELIBERATE TORTURE INFLICTED UPON ANOTHER LIVING BEING.

FOIE GRAS

THERE WAS SOMETHING PSYCHOLOGICALLY WRONG WITH THE 'CHEF' OR 'FARMER' WHO FIRST CONCEIVED A PRODUCT THAT INVOLVES STICKING A PIPE DOWN A BIRD'S THROAT AND FORCE-FEEDING IT UNTIL THE BIRD'S DEATH. I MEAN, THINK ABOUT IT.

VEAL & SUCKLING PIG

YOU REALLY RAN OUT OF THINGS TO EAT, RIGHT? YOU HAVE TO GET TO THE BABIES?

GESTATION CRATES

PIGS ARE HELD FOR BREEDING PURPOSES IN CRATES SO SMALL THEY ARE UNABLE TO LAY DOWN OR TURN AROUND. THEY ARE THERE TO GIVE BIRTH OVER AND OVER AGAIN. THIS INTELLIGENT ANIMAL IS GRADUALLY DRIVEN INSANE AS THE RESULT OF PIG FARMERS' LACK

OF SENSITIVITY AND GREED. JUST IMAGINE AN ENTIRE LIFE SPENT IN A CRATE SO TIGHT YOU CANNOT MOVE.

FUR FARMS & SKINNING

IN SOME COUNTRIES, ANIMALS ARE SKINNED ALIVE, THE FUR PRODUCTS OFTEN SOLD IN THE WESTERN COUNTRIES. CERTAIN REPTILES ARE ALSO SKINNED ALIVE TO MAKE BOOTS AND PURSES. AND DON'T GET ME STARTED ON FUR COATS!

HUNTING

PEOPLE WHO HUNT SHOULD BE HUNTED SO THEY EXPERIENCE WHAT IT FEELS LIKE AND THE USE OF HUNTING DOGS SHOULD BE DISBANDED AS THEY ARE OFTEN DISCARDED AS WELL, ONCE HUNTING SEASON IS OVER.

DOGS ARE TAUGHT TO HUNT BAIT, OFTEN OTHER ANIMALS. OR THE DOGS ARE FED TRAPPED ANIMALS.

ANYONE WHO USES "IT'S MY HERITAGE" AS AN EXCUSE FOR HUNTING IS BEING SELF-DEFENSIVE. THEY SHOULD BE MADE TO DECLARE THEY LOVE KILLING OR HAVE DONE WITH IT.

ANIMAL SACRIFICE

WHETHER WITH BULL-FIGHTING, COCK FIGHTING, DOG FIGHTING OR IN ANY OTHER PRACTICE, THIS DISGUSTING PAST-TIME WAS ALREADY SHAMEFUL IN THE DARK AGES.

DON'T USE THE EXCUSE GOD PUT THE ANIMALS ON EARTH FOR USE BY HUMANS. YOU KNOW HOW THAT HAPPENED PER THE BIBLE? AFTER THE FLOOD, WHEN GOD WISHED TO BRING FEAR TO LIVING CREATURES, INCLUDING HUMANS. BEFORE THAT, THERE WAS NO FEAR. WITH A

PREDATOR, THERE IS FEAR. HOW IS THIS AN IMPROVEMENT IN OUR WAY OF LIFE?

REMEMBER, SERIAL KILLERS AND SADISTS ALWAYS START WITH THE TORTURE AND KILLING OF SMALL ANIMALS AND THEN BUILD THEIR WAY UP THE LADDER OF EVOLUTION.

AQUARIUMS IN FILMS AND TV

HAVE YOU NOTICED THAT EVERY TIME YOU SEE AN AQUARIUM IN THE SCENE OF A TV SHOW OR FILM SOME GUNSHOT OR ACTION WILL SOON RESULT IN SMASHING GLASS AND THE POINTLESS DEATHS OF ALL THAT BEAUTIFUL AQUATIC LIFE? IT'S THAT PREDICTABLE, ISN'T IT?

LOBSTERS

THEY DON'T NEED TO BE BOILED ALIVE. BUT MOST CHEFS CAN'T BE BOTHERED TO KILL THE SHELL FISH CORRECTLY, MAKING THEM NO

BETTER THAN ANY AMATEUR, APPARENTLY. (WITH CRABS THEY OFTEN RIP THEM TO PIECES.)

OTHER CREATURES THROUGHOUT THE WORLD ARE ALSO FRIED OR BOILED ALIVE, WHY I DON'T KNOW. JUST A LACK OF 'HUMANITY' ONE ASSUMES.

REMEMBER, ONCE YOU ARE NO LONGER IGNORANT ON A SUBJECT, YOU ARE RESPONSIBLE FOR YOUR OWN ACTIONS.

AND

THE WORLD'S ISSUES DON'T GET SOLVED WITH PASSIVITY.